Disney
MICKEY & FRIENDS
Go, Team Coco!

By Susan Amerikaner
Illustrated by the Disney Storybook Art Team

First Edition, July 2015
1 3 5 7 9 10 8 6 4 2
ISBN 978-1-4847-0930-6
G942-9090-6-15180

LD90952   03/2015   PRINTED IN USA   LILLY IS A REGISTERED TRADEMARK OF ELI LILLY AND COMPANY. THE QUESTIONS AND ANSWERS AT THE BACK OF THE BOOK ARE COPYRIGHT © LILLY USA, LLC 2015. ALL RIGHTS RESERVED.

Disclaimer: The content of this book is not intended as medical advice. Families should check with their healthcare professionals regarding the treatment of type 1 diabetes.
Content was developed by Disney and reviewed in consultation with Lilly USA, LLC.

Looking for tips on family life with type 1 diabetes?
Visit www.t1everydaymagic.com

What's the Matter with Coco?

It is a hot summer day. Coco and her friends are playing soccer in the park. They are getting ready for the big game!

"Great kick, Coco!" Mickey shouts.

Uh-oh. Goofy is stuck in the soccer net!

Mickey and Minnie help Goofy. Daisy goes to get a drink. She knows it is important to drink water when you exercise. Coco goes, too. She has been thirsty all day!

Coco takes another sip of water. Then she goes back to the game.
Minnie kicks the ball to Coco. Coco dribbles down the field. Oh,
no! Mickey stole the ball.

Coco starts to run after him. Suddenly, she feels very worn out.

Coco sits down on the sidelines. Mickey sits next to her.

"It's really hot today," Mickey says. "Maybe you got too much sun, Coco. Let's get you home so you can cool off."

The next day, Coco's mom calls Mickey. Coco is in the hospital. She didn't get too much sun at yesterday's practice. It turns out she wasn't feeling well because she has type 1 diabetes.

In her hospital room, Coco talks to her parents. "Eeek, eeek," Coco sighs sadly. She is worried. What if the doctor says she can't play soccer anymore? Will her friends still like her?

Coco's parents remind her that the doctor said she can still do everything she used to do. She just needs to plan properly. And her friends will like her no matter what!

But Coco isn't so sure. "Eeek," she sighs softly to herself.

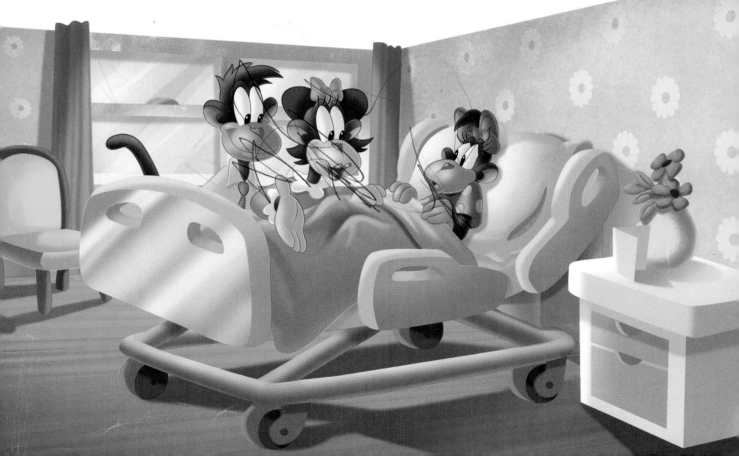

Later that day, Mickey, Minnie, and Goofy come to see Coco. They bring a soccer ball signed by the whole team.

"We thought you could practice here until you can play with us again," Minnie says.

Coco hugs the ball tightly. She hopes she can play soccer with her friends again soon.

Goofy has a gift for Coco, too. It is a stuffed bunny to keep her company.

Just then, Coco's dad comes in. It is time for Coco to learn about diabetes.

Coco waves good-bye to her friends. She is glad they came.

In diabetes class, Nurse Ellie explains what type 1 diabetes is.
"Your body needs fuel to make it work, just like a car needs fuel
to move," she says. "The body's fuel comes from food. In order to
use the fuel and make the car move, you need a key. The body's
key is called insulin. Insulin lets your body use the food you eat
to give you the energy you need to move."

Nurse Ellie explains that because Coco has type 1 diabetes, her
body does not make insulin.

Next Nurse Ellie teaches Coco and her parents how to use a glucose meter to check Coco's blood sugar. Coco chooses which finger to prick. Then Dr. Hill explains what the number on the meter means.

It is time for Coco's insulin. Nurse Ellie teaches Coco's parents what to do. Coco helps by picking where she will get her shot.

Coco's aunt Abby comes to class, too. She wants to be able to help take care of Coco.

Nurse Ellie teaches Aunt Abby and Coco the signs of low blood sugar. "Remember, if you don't feel right, tell a grown-up and have them check your blood sugar," she says. "If you are low, you should drink juice or eat a sugary snack."

Before she leaves, Nurse Ellie gives Coco a bracelet. It says DIABETES. Now people will know what's going on with Coco if she ever needs help.

Coco shows her bunny to Nurse Ellie. "Eeek, eeek." Bunny has type 1 diabetes, too. Can he have a bracelet?

Coco's mom is talking to Dr. Hill. "Eeek! Eeek, eeek!" She is nervous about managing Coco's care at home.

"It seems hard now, but it will get easier," Dr. Hill says. "Remember, we're here to help. And so is Aunt Abby. Coco has a whole team behind her!"

Coco's mom thanks the doctor. She feels better.

Coco hugs Nurse Ellie and Dr. Hill good-bye. It is time to go home.

Later, as her dad pulls up to their house, Coco lets out a happy "EEEK!" Her friends are waiting for her.

"Welcome home, Coco!"

Coco's New Routine

Coco is excited. She got to pick out a supercool backpack to hold her diabetes supplies. It's her favorite color—green! Now she and her dad are filling it with all the things she needs.

Coco's dad picks up her meter. It is time to test Coco's blood sugar.

Coco's mom is on the phone with Nurse Ellie. She has some questions about Coco's diabetes.

Coco looks at her blood sugar number. Then she writes it down in her logbook. Coco likes to help take care of her diabetes by keeping track of her numbers.

"Eeek. Eeek, eeek." Coco reminds her mom that they need to buy snacks at the store.

Later Coco and her mom go shopping. Coco needs supplies for her diabetes bag. She also needs healthy snacks in case she gets hungry.

"Eeek, eeek!" Coco picks out her favorite juice.

Just then, Coco spots Mickey and Goofy.

"Hi, Coco," Mickey says. "We're buying snacks for soccer practice."

"Hiya, Coco," Goofy says. "Look at all the treats I got!"

Goofy runs over with his cart. But he is moving too fast. *Crash!*

"Did I make a goal?" Goofy asks.

"Eeek! Eeek!" Coco explains that Goofy needs healthy snacks for soccer practice. She points to her cart.

"Eeek, eeek, eeek." Eating healthy is important for everyone. Especially when you are exercising. That way you can keep your energy up!

"Gawrsh. I never knew that!" Goofy says.

"Coco's right," Mickey says. "Remember what happened when you had all that soda and candy before practice?"

Goofy remembers falling asleep at practice. "Hyuck. Maybe I *do* need healthier snacks," he says.

"Eeek, eeek." Coco offers to help Goofy find healthy snacks.

"Thanks, Coco. We sure are lucky to have you on our team!" Mickey says.

Goofy sees Coco's mom holding a box of cupcakes. "Those aren't healthy," he says.

"Eeek, eeek," Coco's mom says. Coco can still have sweets on special occasions—like when they win the big soccer game! She just has to plan ahead for them.

It is time for Coco to go home. She invites her friends to come over that afternoon.

Later Coco's friends come to play. Coco shows them the supercool labels she and her mom made for her food.

"Eeek, eeek!" Coco points to her markers and stickers. It's craft time!

While Coco decorates her logbook, her friends draw pictures. Minnie even makes one of Coco playing soccer!

That gives Mickey an idea. "Let's go outside and practice for the big game," he says.

"Eeek, eeek?" Coco asks her mom if she can play.

Coco's mom isn't sure soccer is a good idea. Then she remembers that Dr. Hill said Coco could do all the same things she did before.

"Eeek. Eeek." Coco's mom agrees, as long as they check Coco's numbers before playing.

Mickey and his friends go outside to set up the soccer net. Coco's mom checks Coco's blood sugar to make sure she doesn't need a snack.

"Eeek, eeek." Coco's numbers are where they should be. She can go outside and play.

Coco's parents watch her play in the yard.

"Eeek, eeek," her dad says. He is happy to see Coco having fun.

He knows that diabetes won't hold her back.

Coco's Checkup

Tomorrow is the big soccer game. Coco and her friends are doing drills in the park. Coco's mom reminds her that it is time for her doctor visit.

"Eeek, eeek." Coco is nervous about going to the doctor. She still remembers having to spend the night at the hospital. She would rather keep playing with her friends.

"Gawrsh," says Goofy. "I used to be scared of the doctor, too. But then he gave me this super sticker!"

"We can play again later," Minnie adds.

"Eeek, eeek," Coco's dad says. There is nothing to worry about. Dr. Hill and Nurse Ellie are her friends, too. They are there to help Coco stay healthy, happy, and safe.

Coco nods and gets into the car.

At the doctor's office, Dr. Hill asks how Coco and her parents are doing with her diabetes.

"Eeek, eeek," Coco's mom says. It was hard at first, but they are getting used to measuring Coco's food, checking her blood sugar, and giving insulin. And the whole family is eating healthier and exercising together.

"Eeek, eeek!" Coco tells Dr. Hill that she felt dizzy when she was playing soccer yesterday. Her mom checked her blood sugar and saw that it was low, so Coco had some juice. She doesn't understand why she was low.

Dr. Hill nods. "Lows can be upsetting. They can happen even when you are doing everything right."

Dr. Hill is glad Coco and her mom knew what to do about it.

Dr. Hill examines Coco. She is doing very well.

"Eeek, eeek?" Coco wants to know if she can play in the big soccer game tomorrow.

"You sure can, Coco!" Dr. Hill says. "Just remember to check your blood sugar levels before, during, and after the game to see if you need a snack. And make sure you have your supplies with you."

"Eeek, eeek," Coco's dad says. He and Coco's mom will be there to help.

Coco is so excited! She asks Dr. Hill and Nurse Ellie to sign her soccer ball. After all, they are part of her team, too!

Finally, it is the day of the big game. Coco's mom checks Coco's blood sugar. She is ready to play!

Coco and her friends run up and down the field. Mickey kicks the ball. He scores a goal! The other team scores, too.

At halftime, Coco and her friends eat a healthy snack and drink water to keep their energy up. Coco checks her blood sugar again. She is ready to win the game!

On the field, Coco and her friends chase after the ball. Minnie steals it from the other team and passes it to Coco.

Coco shoots. Score! Coco wins the game for her team!

In the stands, Coco's parents and diabetes team cheer for her. Go, team Coco!

From Coco's World to Yours

Sponsored by

This section provides some simple questions and answers about the story. We hope it will begin a conversation about diabetes, whether you're speaking with a child who has type 1 diabetes, their siblings, or friends. To learn more about diabetes and taking care of diabetes, visit **www.jdrf.org** or **www.diabetes.org**.

What is type 1 diabetes?

Coco has type 1 diabetes. When someone has type 1 diabetes their body doesn't make insulin. Your body needs insulin in order to use the food you eat to make energy. You need energy to do all sorts of things such as reading, running, and playing soccer! Coco takes insulin to replace the insulin her body doesn't make so she can do all the things she loves to do.

What questions do you have about type 1 diabetes?

= Body

= Fuel

= Insulin

What symptoms was Coco experiencing before she found out she had type 1 diabetes?

Coco was tired and very thirsty. These are common symptoms of type 1 diabetes. So are hunger, dizziness, and going to the bathroom a lot.

What symptoms did you have before you found out that you have type 1 diabetes?

Who are the members of Coco's diabetes care team?

Coco has lots of team members. Each one has a special job. Her mom and dad and Aunt Abby help care for her diabetes. So do Nurse Ellie and Dr. Hill. Coco may also meet with a nutritionist to learn about healthy eating.

Who are the members of your team? What job does each one do?

What should Coco do if she is not feeling right?

If Coco is not feeling right, she should tell a grown-up right away and check her blood sugar. Coco could have high or low blood sugar. Everyone has different symptoms when their blood sugar is low, and each low you have may feel different. If you are low, you may feel tired or cranky, you may be hungry, or lots of other things. If you have low blood sugar, you should have juice or a sugary snack. Talk to your doctor about good options for treating low blood sugar.

Sometimes your sugar can be high and sometimes you might just not feel well. If you are high you might need insulin. That is why it is important to figure it out with a grown-up and check your sugar.

How do you feel if you have low blood sugar? How about high blood sugar? What kinds of snacks do you eat if your blood sugar is low?

Why does Coco check her blood sugar?

Coco's parents check her blood sugar levels to see how Coco's eating, activities, and insulin affect her blood sugar. Coco records her levels and the amount of insulin she takes in her logbook. Keeping track of this provides important information to help keep Coco's blood sugar where it needs to be.

Do your parents check your blood sugar (glucose)? Who is responsible for your logbook?

What kinds of foods can Coco eat with type 1 diabetes?

Eating foods that are good for you and not eating too much or too little is important for everyone. Coco likes eating foods that help her stay healthy, such as fruits and vegetables. She also likes eating treats, such as cupcakes, on special occasions. But certain foods are not as healthy as others and can make your blood sugar higher. It's best to plan ahead and only eat those foods sometimes.

Coco's favorite food is bananas. What is your favorite food?

Why is it important for Coco to take her backpack wherever she goes? What supplies should she carry inside?

Coco takes insulin to replace the insulin her body does not make. She also checks her blood sugar to see how her eating, activity, and insulin affect it. Coco needs to eat a sugary snack if her blood sugar is low or if she is very active. When she is away from home, she needs to have all of her diabetes supplies with her. So she puts her blood-glucose meter, lancets, test strips, her insulin, something to eat or drink, her logbook, her parents' phone numbers, and treatment for severe low blood sugar in her backpack.

Do you have a diabetes bag? What do you keep in it?

How has Coco's daily routine changed?

Coco can do everything she used to do, including playing soccer, but now she needs to do a few extra things each day. She has to check her blood sugar before meals and before, during, and after physical activities. She also has to take insulin and carefully select and measure her food. Coco also has to make sure she takes her backpack with her diabetes supplies and snacks in it wherever she goes.

How has your average day changed since you were diagnosed with type 1 diabetes?

Disclaimer: The content of this book is not intended as medical advice. Families should check with their healthcare professionals regarding the treatment of type 1 diabetes.

Content was developed by Disney and reviewed in consultation with Lilly USA, LLC.

Lilly is an expert in type 1 diabetes, and no one knows families like Disney. Now these two companies have come together to create special resources for families like yours.

From Lilly Diabetes and Disney Publishing Worldwide comes a series of books for children of different ages and at varying stages of type 1 diabetes. There's also special content for parents of children with type 1 diabetes on www.t1everydaymagic.com. Visitors to www.t1everydaymagic.com can find articles, videos, recipes, and tips from caregivers raising children with type 1 diabetes. This unique site highlights ways families can establish new routines and let kids be kids. Together, Lilly's deep expertise in type 1 diabetes and Disney's magic can help keep your child and your family feeling inspired and empowered to live a full, active life with type 1 diabetes!

Ask your diabetes healthcare team about getting your hands on the other books in the series and visit www.t1everydaymagic.com!

Also available:

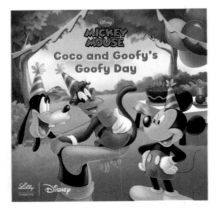